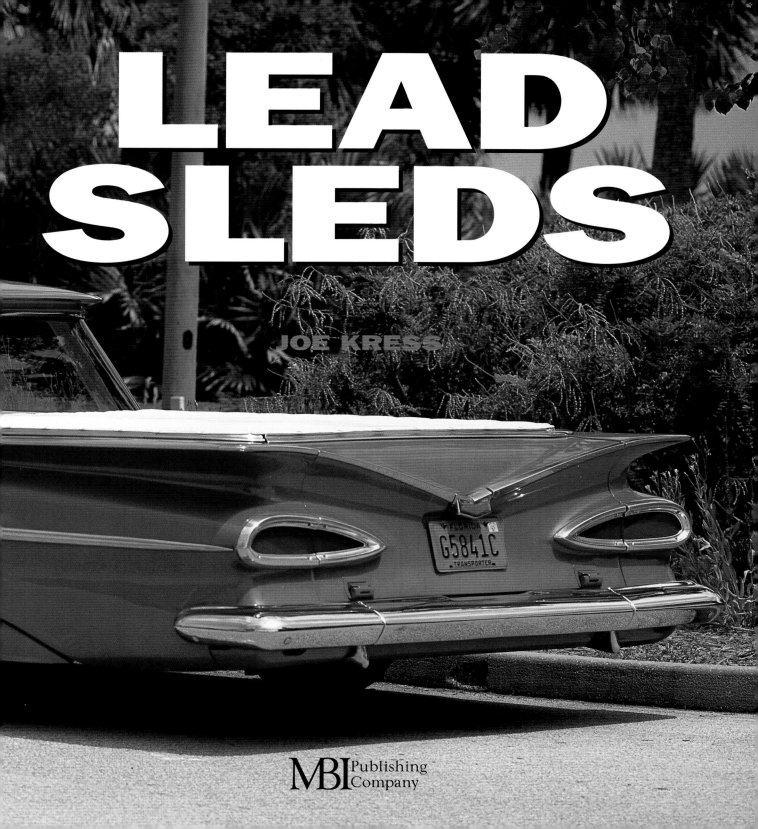

LEAD
SLEDS

JOE KRESS

MBI Publishing Company

First published in 2002 by MBI Publishing Company, Galtier Plaza, 380 Jackson Street, Suite 200, St. Paul, MN 55101-3885 USA

© Joe Kress, 2002

MBI Publishing Company books are also available at discounts in bulk quantity for industrial or sales-promotional use. For details write to Special Sales Manager at Motorbooks International Wholesalers & Distributors, Galtier Plaza, 380 Jackson Street, Suite 200, St. Paul, MN 55101-3885 USA.

Library of Congress
Cataloging-in-Publication Data Available
ISBN 0-7603-1097-1

On the front cover: A scallop-style paint job highlights this '58 Chevy. The chrome-reversed wheels, whitewalls, and fender-well exhaust cut-out are all 1960s era touches. *Mike Key Photo*

On the frontispiece: A little bit hot rod, a little bit custom. Dry lakes-style racing scallops combine with a custom grille bar, tunneled headlights, a shaved bumper, and spinner wheel covers. *Mike Chase Photo*

On the title page: This 1959 El Camino makes a good-looking mild custom. Changes include tunneled-in side pipes, fender skirts, and custom taillight lenses.

On the back cover: Talk about custom styling! Most of the body sculpture of this vehicle comes right from the factory. The dramatic lowering of this Buick enhances the look. *Mike Chase Photo*

About the Author: Joe Kress is an active car enthusiast and has decades of experience in both cars and publishing. He served as an editor at *American Rodder* magazine for 15 years, and is currently an editor at Paisano Publications, as well as a freelance writer and photographer. This is Kress' first book, and he lives in Palm Coast, Florida.

Edited by Amy Glaser
Designed by LeAnn Kuhlmann

Printed in Hong Kong

Contents

Introduction

Customizing is hardly something new. The years immediately following World War II were unquestionably the heydays of the kind of customizing that's still popular today. In its broadest sense, customizing has been around for as long as there have been vehicles to customize. Some of the tricks and techniques that are still in use (pinstriping and the decorative use of gold-leaf trim) got their start centuries ago. They were developed and used to personalize and "customize" carts, carriages, and horse-drawn coaches. When the automobile became popular and took over, it was hardly surprising that the art of customizing would continue. The coach builders and artisans turned their customizing talents to the cars.

Beginning in the 1920s, coachbuilders turned out custom-made automotive masterpieces. These builders included Brunn of Buffalo, New York; LeBaron and Dietrich of Detroit; Walston of Denver, Colorado; and Murphy and Bohman and Schwartz, both of Los Angeles. The factories supplied the builders with bare chassis to create on, and sometimes they did the work directly at the behest of selected, well-heeled enthusiasts. The rich and famous of prewar Hollywood provided a steady flow of customers who wanted to own and be seen in a custom. Widely admired and envied, these customs weren't for everyone. The price was way beyond the means of most.

All this changed in the years immediately following the war. Customizing became available to almost anyone, largely because the work had shifted from those large, prestigious design houses of the 1930s into the hands of individuals laboring in small shops. More important, instead of beginning with a clean sheet of paper for the custom design and hand-crafting completely new bodies to bring these creations to life, the creative touch of automotive customizing was now being applied to production cars. Scores of young, eager bodymen who were freshly released from the armed services and full of desire, ideas, and inspiration took up the torch. Their names are still familiar and are revered today, more than 50 years later. Gene Winfield was a notable postwar customizer. He opened his doors in 1946 and called his Modesto, California, business Windy's Custom Shop. The teams of brothers Gil and Al Ayala, George and Carlo Cerny, and Sam and George Barris all set up shop in and around Los Angeles during the same period. One of the most respected twosomes of those postwar years was Neil Emory and Clayton Jenson. The work that emerged from their Valley Custom Shop in Burbank was stunning. The list of postwar pioneers doesn't end there. Joe Wilhelm, Joe Bailon, and Jack Westergard all put their stamp to this new, everyman's endeavor, and they got enduring results. Bailon is generally credited with the invention of Candy Apple paint, and Westergard's innovative thinking and metal-working skills are still marveled over. Jack Westergard might have been the first man ever to French-in a headlight, fit an Oldsmobile grille into a Mercury's nose, and construct a removable hardtop. During the same period, Glenn Houser's shop in Carson, California, put a twist on that removable-top idea and built padded and upholstered tops that looked amazingly like swept-back and sculpted fold-down convertibles. They were actually one piece and usually solidly mounted. The smooth flowing lines that Houser introduced are copied to this day at a considerably increased price. In the early 1950s, a Carson Top sold for $180.

Each of these innovators developed and honed an individual style and became known for a particular type of custom. The original Barris brothers' style, largely due to the creative eye of Sam, was based on clean lines and simple elegance. Their fade-away fender treatment, a technique that extended the front fenders rearward along the sides of slab-bodied forties-era cars, was a favorite. The Barris look also included long, smooth, curved chopped tops with the lines extending from the top of a lowered roof all the way back to the car's rear bumper. The Barris brothers also made an art form of including just the right amount of chrome trim in just the right places.

Gil Ayala's efforts were equally noteworthy. Ayala's customizing moves were bold. He would swap and graft on completely different fenders and hoods, and he would make other body parts and panels from scratch with raw stock. A 1949 Ayala project was a 1940 Mercury with 1949 Cadillac rear fenders. The front fenders were fade-away that blended into the doors, the top was chopped a full 6 inches, and the car had push-button doors and electric windows.

Practicality wasn't overlooked in the search for style. The practice of channeling a custom's entire body over its frame took hold during the postwar years. This method of lowering a car for a ground-hugging stance retained all the original drivability because the suspension systems could be left untouched. The reasoning: What's the point of having a smooth-looking custom if you have to lift it out of the driveway?

Complete body sectioning was also employed to lower and reshape a custom. This isn't a job for the faint hearted, but the results are dramatic. Essentially the car is cut in half horizontally, and entire sections of the car's sheet metal are removed. When the remainder is reunited, inches lower than before, everything looks different. When the job is done right, the car is better looking. Valley Custom was one of the first shops to routinely employ this extremely difficult technique, and they unfailingly got it right. Emory and Jenson believed that customizing should always make a car more appealing, and the work should enhance the line and the flow to maintain the inherent proportions. To them, this was the essence of customizing. The goal was never to simply make a car different, it was to make it better.

Those ideas and ideals of more than half a century ago still apply, now more than ever. Today customizing is more accessible than in those formative postwar times. Now any enthusiast can take up the torch and the MIG welder and begin to create. Modern tools and materials have made the work easier than ever, and 50 years' worth of techniques have been passed down. Customizing is now open to anyone at just about any budget.

Unlike most other forms of the automotive hobby, a wide range of cars, models, makes, and body types can become the raw material—the empty canvas—for a great custom. Fords, Chevys, Mercurys, Dodges, Buicks, and Oldsmobiles are all fair game. Plymouths and Pontiacs have also been reworked into show stoppers and head turners. Good customs can be crafted from the lowest-priced sedan to luxury cars such as Lincolns and Cadillacs. There is just one rule when it comes to defining what can become a custom. Customizing must make a car better looking, and it doesn't hurt to make the car look cool!

Chapter One

The Classic Customs

Styles of the 1930s, 1940s, and 1950s

A chopped top, slanted doorposts, and custom grille define this Chevy as a classic-style build. Note the spotlights and triple-exit side pipes. *Mike Chase*

In 1952, George and Sam Barris took a year-old Mercury that belonged to a fellow named Bob Hirohata and made history. The *Hirohata Merc* that rolled out of the Barris brothers' shop that year is arguably the most famous custom car ever built in what's come to be known as the classic style. That reworked Mercury was like nothing before it. It elevated the already well-known and, by then, nationally respected Barris style of customizing to a new

and higher level. This vehicle had a new and even smoother look than anything they'd created to that point. For starters, this was the first-ever 1951 Mercury to have its top chopped. That alone would have been distinction enough, but there was a lot more to this particular car. The chosen paint job, and the colors in particular, were a shock to many. Up to this point all customs in general, no matter who had built them, were routinely coated in deep, rich tones. Black and maroon, usually

Above: Rolled and pleated interiors are often seen in classic customs. A late-model steering wheel is a clever addition here. *Mike Chase*

Right: Many end-cap styles are offered to individualize a custom's side pipes. Some enthusiasts even make their own. *Mike Chase*

Left: To many, the definitive classic-era custom is a chopped 1950 Mercury. Details of note include the removed doorposts, Buick side trim, long side pipes, tunneled headlights, and rounded door, trunk, and hood corners. *Mike Chase*

expressed in metallic lacquers, were used often. These were the expected and accepted colors for a custom. This custom's two-tone pale, pastel green paint was a complete about-face and something completely unexpected. By 1953 the *Hirohata Merc* was already appearing on magazine covers and winning first-place awards at car shows across the country.

There's no question that the *Hirohata Merc* set the tone for all classic customs to come. Its

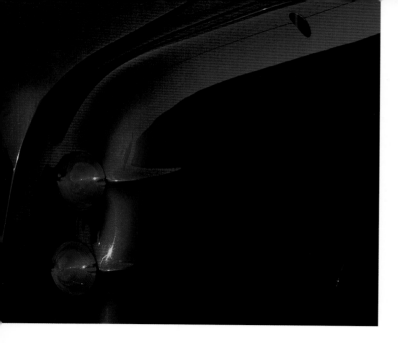

influence has remained as strong as ever right up to today. In addition to its chopped top, this Mercury included the clever addition of the sweeping side trim from an early-1950s Buick—a bright slash of chrome that perfectly divided the car's two-tone paint and lent a streamlined effect that's been copied and mimicked ever since. The car's chopped and stretched top had its doorposts removed. The thick posts were skillfully replaced with gracefully curved pieces of chrome trim to define the window openings. From front to back and top to bottom, the *Hirohata Merc* is a virtual textbook on tasteful customizing in the classic style, even though some of Barris' contemporaries, undoubtedly motivated by envy at what the brothers had created, scoffed at the car and called it overdone. Time and the collective taste of what really works and looks right have proven the naysayers wrong. No one can dispute the correctness of this car's simply elegant

Early Buick taillight lenses have been neatly molded and recessed into this Chevrolet's rear fender. The rounded trunk corner and tunneled antenna are two more classic-era tricks. *Mike Chase*

Customs can go fast too! This early Mercury's flathead V-8 carries all the old-time speed parts, from the triple carburetors to the high-compression heads. Note the alternator and air conditioner, modern concessions to reliability and comfort. *Mike Chase*

An otherwise simple interior receives an eye-popping boost from the custom-stitched headliner and diamond-pleated firewall covering. This is the interior of the legendary *Hirohata Merc*. *Mike Key*

floating grille, scooped quarter panels with the just-visible chrome teeth, or its neatly integrated Lincoln taillights. It all adds up to one of the smoothest custom Mercurys ever built. It's certainly the most famous, and anyone dreaming about and planning to build a custom in the classic style can hardly do better than to carefully study the *Hirohata Merc* and all its nuances and subtleties.

There's little argument that 1949 to 1951 Mercurys epitomize the classic custom. The tops are chopped and correctly proportioned, the doorposts are removed to convert the sedan body into a smoother, flowing hardtop profile, and the already rounded and somewhat stretched bodylines are further exaggerated and visually improved. From every angle and point of view, a Merc is the classic custom in anyone's eyes. To complete the transformation, the cars are often dramatically lowered on their suspensions. That was a job that took a tremendous amount of effort in the 1950s and

often involved extensive frame reworking. Today that element of "the look" is more easily achieved, and with better results, mechanically speaking. For instance, the use of air bag technology allows just about any amount of lowering to be dialed in at the turn of a switch. The range extends from a comfortable and bump-free highway stance to one so ground-scraping low that the car's frame rails are in contact with the pavement.

Pre-1950 Customizing

Customs in this classic style existed well before 1952. In fact, the Barris brothers worked their magic into many earlier-model automobiles before they began reshaping the *Hirohata Merc*. Before the 1949 to 1951 Mercurys became so popular, a lot of 1940s model cars received similar treatments, at least in the sense that they were completely reworked, resculpted, and transformed. Fords, Chevys, Oldsmobiles, and earlier-model Mercurys were routinely chopped, dropped, sectioned,

A Lincoln taillight lens, another classic-era favorite, is smoothly built into the rear fender of a Mercury. Custom work like this, first done in the 1950s, is still popular.

Appleton spotlights have been a popular custom-car accessory for decades. Reproductions are available and originals can still be found. *Mike Chase*

The beginning of the fin era! Pay particular attention to the shape of this Cadillac's wheelwell opening. A curved piece of sheet metal from a 1957 Chevrolet has been grafted in place. *Mike Chase*

A wide, toothy grille is a custom-car classic. Note the rounded hood corners, neatly finished headlights, and the extremely low stance of this Chevy.

Swap-Meet Shopping:
The Custom Car Parts Are All Still There

If you've never been to a giant, no-holds-barred automotive swap meet, you're in for an eye-opening experience. There's nothing like it.

Lately, however, hot rod enthusiasts have had a hard time at the meets. They simply can't find their parts anymore. Swap meets used to be the exclusive shopping store for anyone building an early model hot rod, but the merchandise stock has dried up significantly in recent years. That shouldn't come as a surprise. All of the good bits and pieces needed to put together a car from the 1920s, 1930s, or 1940s have long ago been found, bought up, and are already in use. Hot-rodders, for the most part, are now forced into the aftermarket and must purchase reproductions of things that were once found everywhere.

It's just the opposite for the custom car enthusiast, however. The swap meets are still overflowing with all the desirable parts and pieces. Good, solid, original cars are easily found, priced right, and ready to become the starting point for a custom. For custom-car enthusiasts, swap meets are still a way of life.

There are a couple of explanations for what has become a happy state of affairs for custom-car buffs and a bad turn of events for hot-rodders. First, customs are generally based on cars of the 1950s, 1960s, and 1970s. There's simply more of that stuff still around, and what's around is generally in pretty good shape. Where a hot-rodder would be happy to find a 1934 Ford grille insert in any shape, a grille for a 1963 Chevy is easier to locate, and you can pass up on one or two to search for the perfect example. The same is true for basic body panels, mechanical parts, and interior trim. Customs are made from newer cars, and there are plenty of newer cars and their parts still available in the swap meet.

Swap meets are fertile hunting grounds for customizers. You can find anything from complete cars to start with or just the parts to finish what you already have.

Swap meets are filled with strange and wonderful finds, such as this vintage lead-spraying bodywork set.

become the prime source for hot-rodders has grown into a great secondary source for customizers. You'll find vendors with shelves sagging under the weight of wonderful custom accessories, which are mostly reproductions of classic bolt-ons. From fender skirts to spotlights, lakes pipes to Continental Kits, the custom aftermarket can provide just about any finishing touch you can dream of. Classic wheel covers are standard, and from the Oldsmobile Fiesta to the Cadillac Sombrero, they're all available and brand new.

You'll get a taste of all of this at the swap meets. If you go, you'll come home with great original parts, a few classic reproductions, a pocket full of business cards to file away, and a stack of catalogs to pore over.

Second, there's the matter of make and model. Hot rods, most of them anyway, are Fords. That's the expected marque, so everyone is hunting for the same thing. There simply isn't enough original supply still around to fill that demand. Good customs can be, and are, built from a variety of cars. Any car, from a Chevy to a Cadillac, can, and has been, turned into a dynamite cruiser. The swap meets are packed with stuff for all of these cars.

There is much more than just vehicles to be found at a good swap meet. The aftermarket that has

There's a wealth of custom detail on this one table—everything from tailpipe tips to taillight lenses and spotlights to laminated plastic dashboard knobs. Look closely; there's even a Wolf Whistle!

Racks of fender skirts and an interesting-looking grille offer many possibilities.

17

The *Hirohata Merc* is arguably the most famous classic-era custom ever built. The Barris Brothers constructed this trend-setting car in 1952. *Mike Key*

channeled, smoothed, and restyled by many customizers. In the early 1940s, Jack Westergard and Dick Bertolucci turned their custom creativity to a then virtually brand-new 1940 Mercury Convertible Sedan owned by two brothers from Sacramento, California. Only 970 of this particular hand-built factory model

Mercury were ever produced. This didn't stop the customizers from cutting into and reshaping what was a rare and high-priced, high-end automobile. If anything, the car's rarity and exclusive nature inspired them to dig in and do the factory designers one better and improve the look and line of what amounted to a factory

custom. In place of the standard folding top, Westergard fashioned a flowing, one-piece metal top. It was a removable masterpiece that required the entire rear of the car to be sectioned about 6 inches to allow the top to flow into the trunk area in one uninterrupted line. A 1946 Chevrolet grille was grafted into place, and it fit as perfectly as it did on the car it was taken from for the simple reason that the front section of the Chevrolet hood matching it was grafted into the front of the Mercury's hood. This work was done in 1946 and 1947. Sometime around 1950 this custom received a set of 1948 Ford taillights that were neatly molded into the fenders. Before that change the car had its custom, hand-crafted taillights cut into the bumper guards. Customs, even from the classic era, are never static. When a new idea, a different treatment, or another addition is thought of, it can be implemented. Things on

a car can always be modified even if the car was previously considered complete.

The groundwork that was laid down by the early customizers remains valid to this day. The hardtop treatment on an early 1950s Mercury was, and is, classic customizing at its best. While chopping a top is unquestionably a major undertaking and requires more than a fair amount of metal-working skills, especially when the doorposts and window frames are removed to achieve that hardtop profile, there are countless other small reconstructions that can be completed on other areas of the original sheet metal that will mark a custom as something that was influenced by the work and innovation of the classic era. To lend a smooth line, the car's drip rails can be filled in and gently blended into the lines of the roof itself. On other classic customs, the drip rails are sometimes completely removed. Rounding over every square corner of the hood, trunk lid, and doors is yet another classic technique that is still practiced today. Shaving off and filling in all the car's door and trunk handles and substituting electric solenoids to open the doors is one more common practice with its roots in the classic era. Filling in unwanted body seams, molding in splash aprons for a smooth one-piece appearance, slightly tunneling or recessing a car's headlights into the fenders, and sculpting new taillight surrounds are more examples from the arsenal of customizing tricks and touches that date back five or more decades. The key to a successful custom success, then as it is now, is to combine these changes into a coherent whole that improves

The Westergard/Bertolucci Mercury, another classic-era icon, was built in the 1940s. Its beautifully sloped hardtop is completely handmade, and the grille came from a Chevrolet. *Mike Chase*

A custom painted in classic-era colors. Deep, rich maroons like this were a favorite, along with black and dark blue.

the car's impact, both visually and emotionally. Above all, a custom in the classic style must literally drip with cool.

While a Mercury, specifically any model from 1949 to 1951, is generally considered to be the premier platform to base a classic-era custom on, they are by no means the only ones acceptable. Classic-era customs were crafted from many other makes and models and had equally dramatic results. That's fortunate because the long-standing popularity of those three-year Mercurys has made them somewhat rare today, and when found in good, original condition, or perhaps already customized to some degree, they can be fairly expensive. More than acceptable alternates can be found almost everywhere, and the same effort and similar restyling can be lavished onto one of these completely different cars. It pays off just as handsomely. Sometimes even more so. Indeed, that's one of the great things about the customizing hobby; great customs

These 1956 Packard taillights, a customizing standard, have been mounted upside down. Their lower edge blends nicely with the top of this Oldsmobile's fender.

can be built from almost anything. While fans and participants of other forms of the automotive hobbies might find themselves limited to a small handful of car choices to begin with, a customizer's palette of options is virtually wide open. Great classic-era customs can be made from almost any car manufactured before the mid-1950s. These customs quite often grow out of the most unlikely beginnings, or so it would seem.

Buick: The Donor Car

For many years, Buicks of the early 1950s were usually universally viewed as being not much more than the donors of some interestingly styled small parts that could be incorporated into other, more desirable cars that were being customized. The side trim of a 1953 Buick quickly became a standard on Mercurys, as seen on the Hirohata car. Buick fender portholes were cut out and grafted into the sheet

Next page: Early 1950s Cadillacs have become custom favorites lately. They lend themselves to the customizing art perfectly. *Mike Chase*

metal of other makes. The same was true for the Buick's small, neatly rounded taillights, and they found their way into uncounted customs. Well, all that's still true, with one very important difference: Buicks have finally become recognized as prime classic-era custom material. A 1949 or a 1954 Buick was once hardly given a second look or a second thought, but that's no longer true. Classic-era Buicks are now considered to be almost as desirable as a Mercury. Some customizers prefer Buicks because the coveted side trim, port holes, and taillights are already in place! Looking back just a few more years, Buicks of the immediate postwar period also had the standard fade-away fender lines, with the front fenders extending rearward along the sides of the body all the way back to the beginnings of the rear fenders. In 1949, Buick introduced its Roadmaster Riviera hardtop, yet another custom look straight from the factory that had to be sculpted into many other cars at great expense. By 1950, Buicks were so heavily trimmed with interesting chrome that their front grilles had actually become a massive row of bumper guards, a custom touch if there ever was one. For 1953 the Buick design team outdid itself and released the legendary Roadmaster Skylark sport convertible, a limited-production car that was coveted by restorers. With a current value to reflect that status, it would probably be unwise to change a thing on one of these if it were ever found, other than perhaps lowering the car a bit. Other than the Roadmaster Skylark sport convertible, just about any Buick would make a perfect classic-era custom with minimal effort.

The same holds true for many more overlooked cars of the late 1940s through the mid-1950s. Chevrolets and Pontiacs are two more excellent choices on which to base a classic-era custom. The 1946 to 1948 Chevys were conservatively styled automobiles that lent themselves readily to a customizer's careful touch. With its fade-away front fenders, great stripes of chrome trim as standard, forward-canted doorposts, and gently sweeping fastback roofline, the Fleetline Aerosedan of those years is a custom natural. The peaked, horizontal grille bars Chevrolet used during these years, especially the Stylemaster versions, are so good looking that many customizers routinely incorporate them into other cars. Postwar Chevrolets are extremely popular and are known for being low rider material, but there's no dispute that these cars can be crafted into extremely attractive classic-era customs. The slab-sided body styles of Chevrolets built between 1949 and 1954 offer even more good choices as classic custom bases. During this period, Chevrolet introduced the sporty, two-door hardtop Bel Air models. Even the standard, two-door sedans and business coupes in the Styleline model lines respond well to all types of customizing, especially top chopping with forward-canted doorposts, complete dechroming, frenched and blended headlights and taillights, and the addition of the grille teeth from a Corvette.

Similar in styling to the Chevrolets, the Pontiacs of this time period offer all the same customizing possibilities and a slightly bigger car, which means more up-market comfort, luxury, and detail. The Chieftain Super DeLuxe Catalina, Pontiac's version of the two-door hardtop, is perhaps the most obvious candidate, but Pontiac Torpedo models, Streamliners, and Star Chiefs all offer great possibilities for classic-era customizers.

Moving even further up-scale for a classic-era custom start, Oldsmobiles and Cadillacs through the early 1950s have long been considered customizing favorites. Some of the finest, most refined customs ever built during

Classic-era customs can hide modern drivetrains under their styling. This convertible is comfortably driven thousands of miles every year.

the classic era were Oldsmobiles. Even today, an 88 or 98 Series Holiday hardtop coupe is a wonderful choice for customizing, and the Oldsmobile possibilities hardly end there. The sedans and convertibles are filled with great styling and factory detailing that beg to be enhanced at a customizer's hand. The Cadillac Eldorado model, first seen in 1953, was directly derived from the GM Motorama parade of futuristic car designs. It doesn't take an Eldorado to make a perfect classic-era custom. Fleetwoods, Series 62 fastback sedans, and Coupe DeVille models are all wonderful examples of classic-era customs just waiting to

be altered. By 1949, Cadillacs sported the beginnings of their trademark tail fins, a body panel that's often been transferred intact to other cars, especially Chevrolets.

Building a custom to the classic-era style is a worthy endeavor for a number of reasons. These chopped, canted, streamlined, dechromed, frenched, filled, lowered, tunneled, and recontoured cars are the vehicles most often recognized as "customs," and their allure is as strong as ever. Correctly done, which really means correctly proportioned, a classic-era custom is an American icon. What more could any customizer ask for?

Chapter Two

The Swinging 1960s

Custom Cars in a Changing America

Under all this custom work there's a 1956 Oldsmobile, although not many people may recognize it now. The restyle is complete from front to back.

While there are many who might believe that the "classic era" defines everything that's good and true about custom cars, feeling that the restyling and creativity born during the 1940s and 1950s is not exactly true and it is certainly not the end of the custom-car story. Custom cars built in the the 1960s, and customs built today to look as though they were built then, are just as viable and desirable as a style. That's particularly true for many customizers today, and it's all a matter of the customizer's age.

Nostalgia comes in many forms and time frames. While the customs of the 1940s and 1950s are certainly widely celebrated, re-created, and restored, the work today is being done and the traditions are carried on by custom-car enthusiasts who quite likely might not have even been alive during the style's heyday. Or if they were, they were undoubtedly much too young to have actively participated with original customs of their own. When we realize that customizing's classic era took place 50 years ago, and the customizers active during the period were young men in their 20s and 30s, it's not hard to understand why most classic-era customs today are being built or restored by people paying homage to a time and a style they personally had no real,

Later-model bucket seats and a custom console that are upholstered to complement the body color offer up an inviting and comfortable interior. *Mike Chase*

Left: Talk about custom styling! Most of the body sculpture of this vehicle comes right from the factory. The dramatic lowering of this Buick enhances the look. *Mike Chase*

hands-on involvement in. It is rare to see a 70- or 80-year-old still active in the custom car field. Customs of the 1960s, however, are an entirely different matter.

The 1960s, and the early to mid-1970s, was the coming-of-age period for the post-war Baby Boomers. For many Boomers the custom cars of the 1960s aren't just something envisioned from afar or perhaps read about in history books and old magazines. They are the cars from times that were lived during the most formative years of life. It's

little wonder why today many of these same people are now at a point in their lives where they have the time and resources to indulge themselves and revisit the best times of their life. Those times included some great custom cars that were built to a style that's still as much fun now as it was originally. It may be even more so because enthusiasts of that era are now in a position to build and complete the custom car that they never got quite right the first time around. The chance to rewrite personal history doesn't come often, and

Custom-car detail doesn't stop under the hood. Plenty of chrome and braided stainless steel brighten up this engine compartment. *Mike Chase*

Mild dechroming highlights are all that's left in place. In this case, what's left are some very interesting hood and fender lines. *Mike Chase*

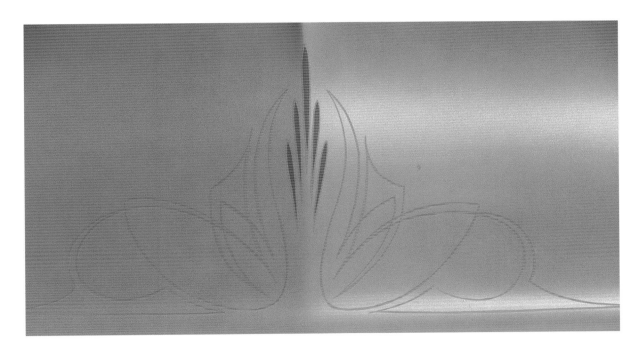

Pinstriping can be simple or it can be extremely ornate. This kind of customizing dates back centuries to the days when horse-drawn carriages and carts were the mode of the day. *Dain Gingerelli*

many custom-car enthusiasts will take full advantage of this.

From a cultural and historical viewpoint, the 1960s were actually two very distinct and very different times—a pair of decades both somehow contained in a single, 10-year period. The first half of the 1960s was very much a continuation of what came before. It was a national and cultural time of innocence carried over, almost unchanged, from the 1950s. The popular image of these years came with a soundtrack made up of good-times Beach Boys surf music, and the carefree fun-in-the-sun frolicking depicted in a string of Frankie and Annette beach-blanket movies. The custom cars of the early 1960s fit neatly into all of this, and actually didn't differ all that much from what had been created just five or seven years earlier. All of the customizing styles of the 1950s—the top-chopping, body-sectioning, channeling, tunneling, frenching, and rounding over—continued on with one very important, yet subtle, difference. There was just less of it going on. By the mid-1960s custom cars and most forms of the car hobby had begun falling out of favor. The times, as Bob Dylan sang, were changing.

Next page: The longer, lower, and wider craze began in 1958, and this Pontiac is the perfect example. Simple grille work and air-brushed graphics make the car a head-turner today. *Dain Gingerelli*

Cadillac "bullet" taillight lenses are an effective addition to this 1958 Chevy. These lenses are often tunneled into fenders.
Mike Key

The second half of the 1960s couldn't have been more different than the first. It was a period of unprecedented social upheaval that unraveled all the tranquillity that preceded it. These were the years punctuated by the Vietnam War and the youth protests that the global conflict spawned. All that earlier surf music and all the syrupy boy-meets-girl movies were gone. They were replaced by acid rock, psychedelic music, and counterculture films such as *Easy Rider*. Custom cars and most forms of the auto hobby seemed to gradually disappear until it seemed they were completely gone. For many, floral-design Volkswagen mini-buses became the motorized statement of choice. They were used as personal proclamations that rapidly took the place of the customs from an earlier time, a time that actually wasn't all that long past. There were customs in the second half of the 1960s, but there just

Chrome, chrome, and even more chrome! This engine compartment detail includes period-correct firewall decals.
Mike Key

This bright interior treatment has been executed with color-matching paint, upholstery, and chrome. Note the teardrop-style plastic control knobs. *Mike Key*

weren't all that many. By the end of the decade, custom cars might just as well have been invisible. The auto factories of Detroit, along with all those societal changes, were part of the blame for the lack of hand-crafted, custom cars on the highways and at the drive-ins.

Catering to an emerging youth market, America's automobile industry responded with something that was both quicker and easier, in every sense of those words. A full assortment of musclecars began to appear. These cars offered speed, power, and style, and it all came at an affordable price and was packaged with readily available, easy-credit payments. The popularity of another new automotive category, the "pony cars," created for this new youth market took off like a shot after the 1964 introduction of the Ford Mustang. With these flashy new cars, custom cars just didn't seem relevant. Yet, there were still some great customs of the 1960s and early 1970s, and building to that style today is just as rewarding now as it was then.

continued on page 44

Custom Construction:

Big Shop or Back Alley Garage, The Aim is the Same

Sooner or later you're going to get your hands dirty. If you're customizing on a budget, count on it being sooner than later. Nothing in this hobby comes at a higher price than professional labor charges, so the more you can learn to do yourself, the more you'll save. That's obvious. What's not so obvious is the enjoyment and personal satisfaction that comes from being able to say, "I did it myself" when some admirer comments on and asks about this modification or that clever adaptation once your custom is done and on display at its first cruise night. No price tag can be put on that.

It doesn't take a pro's workshop full of specialized tools and equipment to create some pretty special work, either. A basic set of hand tools, a few bodyworking hammers and dollies, a bench vice, drill press, and a grinder will get you started. An inexpensive 110-volt MIG welding outfit, a good air compressor, and a decent paint-spraying gun will take you the rest of the way. As you get into the project, you'll discover that you have a knack for this bit of work or that technique, and you'll want the specialized tools and pieces of equipment that make the jobs easier and have better results. The catalogs from the Eastwood Company are filled with quality tools and shop equipment that are aimed at the hobbyist, and it's all sized and priced accordingly.

To avoid discouragement and custom-car burnout, start slow and keep the jobs simple. Then, as your skills progress, move into the more complex jobs. That's the way the pros approach a project, and it's the way anyone should, especially a first-timer. Keep in mind that before any car can be customized, it must first be put back into good, original condition. Begin by replacing rusted panels with new metal (patch panels and

Let the sparks fly! For many, building a custom is just as much fun as driving one.

Far Left: A classic custom in the making. This Chevy is a long way from being done, but it's already showing its potential.

The weld-stitching on this just-chopped roof looks rough, but with grinding and filling it will soon disappear into a new, better-looking profile.

A Cadillac taillight has been grafted into a Chevrolet fender. Modern, low-cost shop equipment allows anyone to attempt this kind of work.

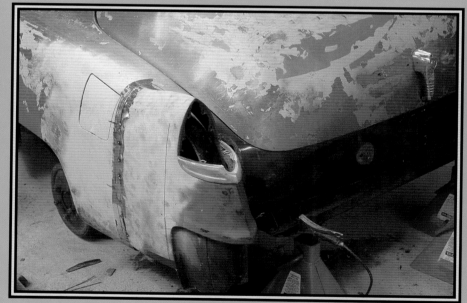

even complete body sections are readily available for most cars that are custom candidates). Using your basic body hammers and dollies, work out all the dings and dents. You're not wasting your time, even if you later end up cutting away some of this restoration repair to make way for a custom touch. At the very least you'll be getting acquainted with your tools and equipment and honing the skills that will come into play when

you've moved on to chopping the top, sectioning the body, tunneling the headlights, frenching the taillights, and relocating the fender arches.

That last list sounds intimidating, doesn't it? Chopping a top is a major undertaking, but it isn't

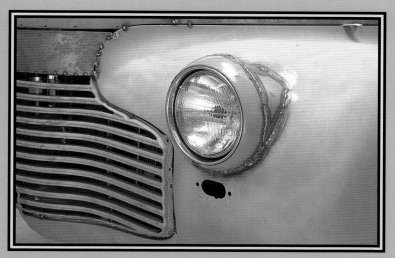

This is a by-the-numbers frenched and extended custom headlight job. The rim is a reproduction 1952 Mercury part. Custom-formed sheet metal that was cut from a template connects it to a 1941 Chevy fender.

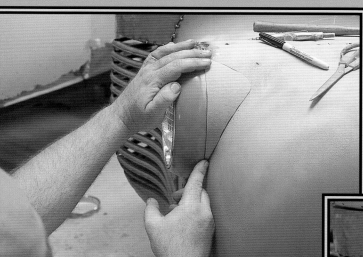

all that difficult. It's nothing more than bodywork, and with practice it will seem no more difficult than a simple rust repair. In truth, the hardest part of all in chopping a top correctly, or doing any other major modification for that matter, is being sure that the work actually improves the car's look and its line. That takes a practiced eye as much as anything else. Remember, the goal of customizing is to make a car better, not just different.

Continued from page 37

Customs in the 1960s and 1970s

The traditional early 1960s custom is very much a 1950s style with one very important distinction: All the extensive body reshaping that was common in the 1940s and 1950s, the top chopping and sectioning, was minimal. Instead, the sheet-metal work was often restricted to a tasteful minimum. Many times it was limited to simple dechroming and the removal of door and trunk handles. Custom taillights might have been fitted, with the favorites being 1956 Packard peaked lenses grafted into rear fenders, and the entire rear fenders of early 1950s Cadillacs were commonly spliced into Chevrolets of the same era. The ever-popular 1959 Cadillac bullet taillight lenses found themselves added onto and tunneled into custom cars of all makes, models, and styles. Subtle frenching of the radio antenna was almost mandatory, and headlights

Full wheel covers are a custom-car tradition. These spinners work well with thin-line whitewall tires.

Previous page: This 1959 El Camino makes a good-looking mild custom. Changes include tunneled-in side pipes, fender skirts, and custom taillight lenses.

A 1956 Packard taillight lens tops off a fender that's been extended almost a foot!

were blended and molded into fenders and often retained a chrome trim ring. Custom grille work was also popular, and the styles here ranged from the sublime to the downright silly. The very best front-ends of the time often featured the multitooth look of highly chromed and polished Corvette grille bars or trimmed-down Packard or DeSoto parts neatly fit into new applications. Right alongside this careful and well-thought-out work was the awful practice of filling a grille opening with a panel of expended metal and then bolting on an assortment of chrome-plated kitchen cabinet door handles. That's a style best left alone and forgotten to history, even though some builders, including some professionals, attempted to refine the look by

using short lengths of round or oval tubing in place of the hardware-store ornaments. It didn't work then, and it doesn't work now.

The Ground-Scraping 1960s

Sixties-era custom cars were low. Extremely low. The common look was a ground-scraping stance with the side pipes or the rocker panels just clearing the pavement. Of course, actually driving these cars presented certain problems, but that was dealt with during this decade too. It was during the 1960s, albeit in the latter part of the decade, when hydraulic suspension systems first began showing up on certain custom cars. These adjustable systems—made up of pumps, rams, and jacks, adapted into and onto a suspension system altered with shortened coil springs—allowed a custom car's ride or show height to be varied by raising or lowering the entire car, or either end of it separately, at the touch of a button. Today these systems are most often associated with lowriders, but customs had them first.

In the 1960s many custom cars served as a transition from the customs of the 1950s and the glitter-painted ground scrapers of the 1970s and 1980s. The wild and radical sheet-metal alterations so common in the 1950s were being replaced with wild, and often radical,

Next page: A scallop-style paint job highlights this 1958 Chevy. The chrome-reversed wheels, whitewalls, and fender-well exhaust cut-out are all 1960s-era touches. *Mike Key*

These scallops are more than paint; they are now part of the body. They've been outlined with thin tubing and filled in with sheet metal.

paint jobs. Metalflake and pearl topcoats in a variety of colors took the place of the 6-inch chopped tops of an earlier time. In many cases, the effect of the paint job was, and can still be, just as stunning. The overall impact is just as strong as what had been created earlier with large amounts of sheet-metal recontouring. All of this is possible largely because of the design of the cars that are now being customized. Perfect examples of this new style of customizing are the Chevrolets from the mid- to late 1950s. The paint, mild de-chroming, and subtle add-on treatment on a 1958 Chevy was so popular that one was prominently featured in the movie *American Graffiti*. The sculpted, flowing lines of just about any automobile that was designed

and produced from the mid-1950s and on lent themselves perfectly to this new, easy, and inexpensive style of customizing.

Some time around 1957, Detroit's stylists began working in what could be termed their "fin era." There was more than just adding height and dimension to the rear fenders of the previously slab-sided cars that were manufactured. Every panel of the cars' bodies received new attention at the drawing board. The result was a completely new look. This was a look and style that played perfectly for customizers seeking to personalize their cars. The 1958 Chevrolet was just a beginning of what was to come. Chevrolet's 1959 designs, heralded in dealer brochures of the time as being "all new, all over again," featured body designs that were even more controversial than the look of the cars produced just one year earlier. Especially disconcerting to some were the wide, broad, horizontal tail fins that debuted that year, as well as the dramatic increase in the overall size of the 1959 cars as a whole. What appeared to be glaring, overdone, and excessive to the eyes of some, this new look and style was almost a dream come true for a customizer, and that was just the Chevrolets. Most of the cars produced during the mid- to late 1950s and the early part of the 1960s exhibited some form of exaggerated styling right from the factory. This included cars from General Motors, Ford, and Chrysler. The customizers had honed and perfected techniques of simple dechroming, trim and handle removal, lowering, and painting. These techniques became a perfect match to these new platforms of automotive personalization, especially the painting.

With a practiced eye, custom painters took the factory styling, and with the skillful application of scallops, flames, pinstriping, and full body panels painted in contrasting colors, they emphasized and highlighted the work of the designers in Detroit. Larry Watson, who worked in the Los Angeles area, became one of the better known practitioners of this style of painting, but he was certainly not alone. Customizers from coast to coast were learning quickly that paint alone could dramatically transform almost any one of these already highly stylized Detroit stockers into a flashy, head-turning, eye-popping custom. The experience of Larry Watson himself, working on his own 1959 Cadillac coupe, is a perfect illustration of the possibilities available. Watson purchased a brand-new Cadillac and drove the car directly from the dealer's showroom to a local bodyshop. There, the chrome trim was removed from the hood and trunk lid and the outside door handles were taken off. Next, a suspension shop lowered the new car by cutting a few coils out of the springs. That was the extent of the physical changes made to the car. Watson then repainted the Cadillac in his signature panel-paint style and mixed a pearl white with a vivid, ruby candy color paint. The car was driven and shown for many years and had high acclaim. No one cared or commented that the real customizing, the basic style of the car, came directly from Cadillac.

The 1960s began as a continuation of the 1950s and ended as something completely different. Customizing in the 1960s style can sometimes seem as schizophrenic as the decade itself. Today, a customizer has the choice of either emulating the earlier years of that decade, when a custom car included a somewhat refined look that was essentially the

The classic 1960s style is still classic today. The contrasting piping adds interest to this all-white interior.

same as what was seen in the 1950s, or jump ahead to the closing years of the 1960s when paint jobs and lowered suspensions became the defining trends. Either choice is valid and is a correct interpretation of customizing during the 1960s, a period when the times were definitely changing.

Chapter Three

Staying Stock, or So It Would Seem

Customizing Cars the Designers Got Right

Cadillacs like this are gaining favor fast. Customizers love the crisp, sharp lines that are accented here with a wild flame-paint job. *Mike Chase*

Customizers today have the luxury of being able to look back over a rich history of customizing and choose the style or time period that pleases them the most. Sometimes that means choosing a car that already has inherently interesting lines and looks straight from the factory and leaving that car's sheet metal alone. Call it restoration-customizing, if you will. The process is a basic cleanup to repair all the dings and dents, lower the car just a little, and apply a coat of fresh, new paint. It can work wonders and turn heads.

A quick look through the automotive offerings of Detroit during the late 1950s and continuing on up through the early 1970s would show any number of interesting, enthusiast cars that a modern customizer could take and make into a personalized statement of style and taste with minimal effort. It doesn't always

The white rolled-and-pleated upholstery of this DeSoto is set off with body-color accents. Dice as control knobs bring a smile too. *Dain Gingerelli*

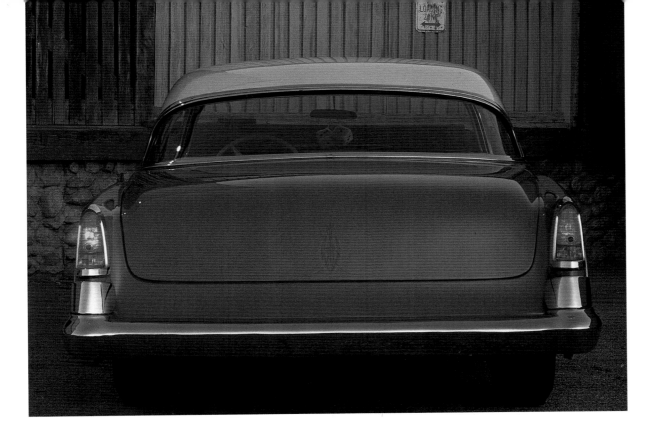

A dechromed trunk lid and shaved-clean bumper are accented with just a touch of pinstriping. Effective customizing isn't always the result of extensive bodywork. *Dain Gingerelli*

require massive amounts of specialized bodywork to come up with a car guaranteed to generate a splash on the highways and turn heads at the drive-in cruise nights. Sometimes all that "heavy lifting," or hard work, has already been done at the factory level. All that's required is a good eye to spot the right candidate, and then the application of just a little custom-car savvy to make that factory custom even better.

Beginning in the mid-1950s every automaker in Detroit produced a full lineup of cars where almost any one falls into this category of the least costly, but often most rewarding, style of customizing going on today. The sculpted, exaggerated lines originally penned in every design studio in Detroit were wild-looking and, in many cases, too wild for the somewhat conservative tastes of the time. But they're perfect for a modern customizer seeking a modern custom. Left almost in original condition, the designs that once might have seemed outrageous and even a little over-the-top, are now just right to a customizer's eye.

continued on page 59

Next page: Great cruise-night customs are not always what is expected in a custom. This eye-popping DeSoto would be a winner anywhere. *Dain Gingerelli*

Cruise Nights:
Going Local for Custom Car Fun

No one will ever argue the claim that cruising into a giant custom-car convention staged by one of the big national clubs such as the KKOA or the West Coast Kustoms is an experience that must be lived to be believed. Spending a week, or just a long weekend, in a far-away town filled with customs of every description is wonderful fun. Nowhere else will you find lead sleds and customs in such concentration. A custom car "Big Run" usually includes a large commercial exposition showcasing everything currently available from the custom-car aftermarket, and it gives you a firsthand look at the work of legendary

Local cruise nights are the perfect, low-key ticket to custom-car fun.

A 1951 Ford with a new admirer. Cruise nights expose customs to everyone, and often someone who is just looking returns to the next show driving a custom!

professionals. In addition, you just might uncover that Pontiac grille bar or Packard taillight you've been searching for. All that and more is included in a national run; they're a big part of the hobby.

Albeit on a smaller scale, a lot of that same sort of fun is going on right around the corner weekly. Look for car shows, and you will find plenty of custom-car action close to home. In some parts of the country, it happens as often as every night of the week. Good custom-car runs are being held in your

own hometown, or maybe just over into the next county, which is even better because that means there's an hour or two of custom cruising involved.

These car events are called "cruise nights," and the small, and sometimes not so small, local gatherings are the real backbone of the custom-car hobby. A cruise night is the perfect excuse to get out, drive, enjoy a custom, and meet other customizers.

Informal or well-orchestrated cruise nights are everywhere. They range in size from just a handful of

future cruise nights to attend for as often as you care to fill the tank.

At a local cruise night, you'll be among others who appreciate a nicely frenched headlight and smoothly chopped top. You'll probably discover new favorite restaurants and hangouts too. By mapping out and exploring interesting roads that lead to new cruises, you'll find local sites and stops you never knew existed. Most important of all, you'll be out on the street with a custom. Once your custom is finished, or even if it isn't, check out the local cruise scene. You won't regret it.

A 1961 Impala convertible draws approving glances. Rods, customs, and classics all show up at a local cruise.

cars to hundreds of them. Thousands, even, as can be the case when an older, established cruise celebrates an anniversary. Local cruise nights usually don't have any rules either, which means if it's interesting chances are you'll see it. Cruise nights throw out the welcome mat to everyone: hot rods, late-models, motorcycles, sports cars, and a lot of customs.

Finding a cruise night is easy. Look for flyers at local speed shops, accessory stores, and parts suppliers or announcements in the local newspaper's classified sections. Word-of-mouth recommendations often lead to the best cruises; find and attend just one cruise night and you'll have all the information you need on

A town will often block off its entire downtown for a cruise. It makes for a pleasant car show and evening out.

The color-matched checkerboard pattern painted inside this spinner wheel cover is the kind of detailing an almost-stock custom requires. *Dain Gingerelli*

Continued from page 53

Customizing to this style, which really means customizing with details (with some notable exceptions, which we'll get to a little later), dictates that the chosen car is to be selected with extreme care. When the overall line, and most or all of the original trim, are going to be left untouched, except for a careful restoration, the lines and trim had better be the right stuff. Rest assured, the right stuff is readily available, and it's not always the obvious choices that make the most interesting cars to customize with the light touch. Many know that a 1959 Cadillac convertible is pretty much the last word in factory excess

and is a car that doesn't need a thing. It doesn't mean that it's the last word for customizers, though. There are many other equally interesting possibilities to pick from, and because they're not the obvious choices they're not so expensive to begin with. It's a real consideration for a customizer on a budget. Cars of the Chrysler Corporation are often overlooked for their custom potential. For the adventurous customizer, there's a gold mine of sheet metal to be worked on Chryslers.

By 1957, which is right around the beginning year for factory cars that can become customs with little change, Virgil Exner's design

This 1957 Ford tailfin and taillight appear to be stock, yet both have been completely reworked to add interest to the original lines. This is tricky! *Mike Chase*

Fury is one of the most interesting automobile designs to ever come out of Detroit. The 1960 models retained the exaggerated tailfins introduced in 1957 and added a sculpted front-fender cove outlined with chrome trim that extended over the headlights and onto the hood. This was a look that customizers of years past had never dreamed of, and if they had, it would have taken untold hours of very skillful and complicated metal reshaping to achieve. Yet here it is, direct from the factory. The rarely customized DeSoto Firedome and Fireflite models offer the same stunning results in a somewhat subdued guise. It's subdued once you get past the shocking colors these cars were sometimes delivered in. The chrome trim added onto De-Sotos and all Chrysler cars perfectly lent itself to becoming the dividing line between two-tone paint jobs. The stylists of the time didn't leave it at that. They often worked in a third accent color to make the cars three-toned. Bright yellow and black, or various shades of aqua or magenta or purple combined with rich whites or creams were common. The colors were eye-popping even then, during a time when bright colors were everywhere and routinely showed up even on kitchen appliances and dinnerware, imagine the response one of these cars would generate today. Pull in any-where driving a 1958 DeSoto Fireflite Adven-turer convertible with three-toned paint gleaming and chrome trim glistening, and there won't be a head that doesn't turn or a face that doesn't break into a broad grin. It's almost a guarantee.

team at Chrysler had really hit its stride. All through the corporation's lineup and in all of its various divisions, the cars were colorful, full-fledged members of the "tailfin and chrome" school of design. For example, a 1957 through 1960 Plymouth Belvedere or

Customizing the Cadillac

A 1959 Cadillac is a desirable car when it comes to restoration customizing, but there are other model years just as desirable as that 1959, although it's a safe bet that Cadillacs produced earlier than 1959 won't be found at giveaway prices. A 1957 Eldorado Brougham, for instance, was a $14,000 car when it was new. Its airplane styling was packed with every conceivable option and loaded with power features never before seen on a car. That's a collector car, period. Early 1950s Cadillacs offer a lot of possibilities, as do the post-1959s. With their crisp, clean lines, especially on the 1961 models, Caddys in general carried on with the late 1950s flair, but in a more sophisticated vein. The tailfins came down slightly, as did the overall size of the cars themselves, and the sculpted body panels started to take the place of chrome trim. By the mid-1960s, Cadillac tail fins had disappeared completely and were replaced by long, low, sweeping cars that are perfect for a modern customizer's cruise-night

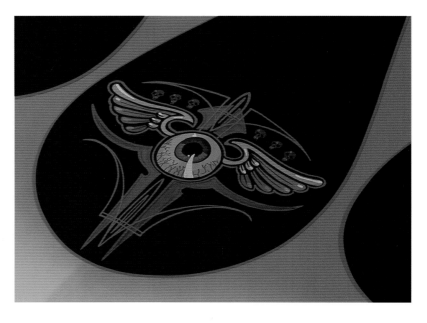

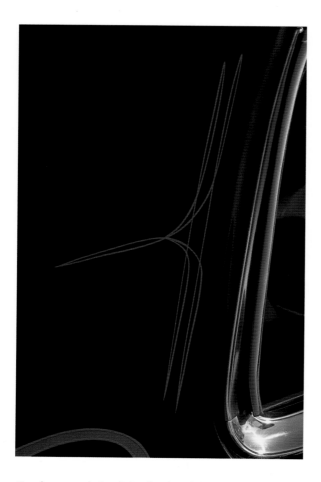

Here's an example of simple pinstriping. Customizers have favored accents like this for years. *Mike Chase*

thing for car buyers of the time and were pretty much a sales failure, all that chrome looks good today.

Buick released yet another new car with a completely new look for 1959. It featured exaggerated tailfins and sculpted bodylines. The 1960 models continued on in this excessive direction, but this time it came straight from the factory with what looked like a custom bullet grille. After this, most full-size Buicks became a bit more trimmed down, cleaned off, and less interesting for modern purposes, with one giant exception. In 1963, Buick introduced the Riviera, a four-seat sports car that became an immediate classic. A Riviera is a custom straight off the showroom floor. Its top appears already chopped, and the grille, fenders, headlights, and roof flow in a clean, crisp line. Rivieras need nothing to be beautiful, yet modern customizers still manage to make them better. Sometimes the car is simply lowered, other times the customizing is more extensive and goes to the point of actually chopping more off the top. The effect is stunning and dramatic, yet any Buick that has been lowered, repaired, repainted, and detailed is a bona fide stunner.

The same sort of look and result can be found in other General Motors brands manufactured during the mid-1950s through the mid-1960s. Oldsmobile, Pontiac, and Chevrolet all offer excellent choices for a customizer planning to leave the basic sheet metal, for the most part, intact. If the most chrome trim for the dollar is desired, it's hard to surpass 1958 models. The chrome went on by the pound. Tall and wide tailfins began the next year, and by the early 1960s, the lines started to noticeably clean up and crisp up.

The Ford Motor Company certainly shouldn't be overlooked here, either. While Fords of these same years were a bit more

special. When lowered on its suspension, a 1960s-era Caddy is tough to beat.

Everything said about the Cadillacs also applies to other General Motors products, Buick in particular. While the Buicks from the early to mid-1950s fit better into the classic-era mold, by the end of the 1950s and well into the 1960s Buick made some outrageously styled automobiles. The 1958 models were as over-chromed as anything made in Detroit. While they proved to be too much of a good

A big, roomy interior is another plus to customizing a mid-1960s car. Later-model seats have been fit into this vehicle. *Mike Chase*

restrained in their styling, there are also definite FoMoCo possibilities offered. Primarily, the most impact will come from one of Ford's upscale models, such as a Thunderbird. For a touch of luxury cruising, a Lincoln is the best choice. Both models are beautifully designed automobiles.

No explanation is needed to describe the popularity of 1955, 1956, and 1957 T-birds. These two-seaters are genuine American classics and are most often saved for total and factory-correct restorations. Yet some are customized, and to good effect. The 1958 Thunderbird, the so-called "square bird," is the basis for a quintessential early 1960s custom and the perfect platform for a panel-paint job. By 1961, Ford had introduced a third-generation

Thunderbird, which was yet another styling masterpiece. By that time, the Thunderbird was a large, personal-luxury car, in both coupe and convertible guise. A T-bird of this era is a head-turner anywhere. Ford even offered its own customizing options for the T-Bird during these years. In late 1961, Ford introduced the Sport Roadster version, a two-place conversion made possible by a fiberglass tonneau cover over the rear seats. This accessory piece began at the rear deck and extended forward to include a pair of sculpted headrests. Chrome wire wheels completed the package, and make no mistake, that very same package is a cruise-night winner today. Even more luxurious were the Lincolns of these same years, most especially the Continental models. It would be hard

to find a more sculpted automobile body than what appeared on 1958 and 1959 Lincolns. The cars were magnificent in their excess with their canted headlights, sharp bodylines and fender fins, and heavily chromed grilles. By 1960 the look had been cleaned up significantly, and the 1961 models were wonderfully simple in their execution. Crisp, flat-sided lines replaced the whimsical coves and curves seen just a few years earlier. Some models even featured suicide-(reverse) opening rear doors. Besides offering style in a number of tastes, Lincolns built during these years were extremely well constructed. Each car was road tested before it left the factory.

To this point we've been considering cars that require, and receive, no special metal work, other than repair, to become an interesting and valid custom choice. Lately there have been a few exceptions to this rule. Certain cars of the era are being subtly reshaped to better express the designers' original intent. On these cars a fin might be extended by another fraction of an inch, or a bodyline is slightly deepened. At a glance the car looks stock, but somehow it seems just a little better. Needless to say, this kind of work is extremely expensive to purchase, and because of that it is mostly limited to the discerning, high-end enthusiast. The fact that the changes being made are all minute additions says something important about what's already there. Sometimes the factory designers got it right the first time.

This 1957 Ford Ranch Wagon looks almost stock. It's anything but stock, and the recontouring is so subtle it almost goes unnoticed. *Mike Chase*

Chapter Four

Custom Rods and the Mild Style

A Little Bit Hot Rod, A Little Bit Custom, A Whole Lot of Fun

This is another example of stock styling left alone. This late 1940s convertible has plenty of class already.

It's

a local Friday-night cruise and a chopped-top 1951 Mercury that's been covered in about a thousand coats of deep maroon candy paint rolls in. It's dressed out with fender skirts, long side pipes, and a Corvette grille. This is a gorgeous machine, but you can bet that slicked-down Merc won't stay in the starring role all night long. Before too much time has passed some other car will roll in, something completely different and built to a completely different style. It might be a 1960s-era piece, maybe a 1958 T-bird lowered to the pavement on its hydraulics and sporting a triple-tone lime green-and-white-and-gold panel-paint finish. All attention will immediately shift over to this newcomer. It happens all the time, and it won't be because the original hit-of-the-night missed any tricks or its builder cut some corners during the makeover. Instead it will be just custom-car business as usual, where anything goes, styles change, and tastes vary. It's a custom-world guarantee that there will be something for everyone.

Cars modified in the style of custom rods are an interesting mix of themes, and that is what makes these cars so popular. A custom rod is exactly what its name implies, a car that's not exactly a custom in the strictest sense of what that means, and it is not a hot rod either. Instead, it's a blending of the two. A hot rod incorporates more than a little custom styling and common customizing techniques, and a custom includes a healthy helping of hot rod parts, aesthetics, and "feel." The resulting custom rod can win the admiration of both customizers and hot-rodders alike when it is done correctly, but more than that, it is welcomed into events or gatherings that might otherwise be restricted to one aspect of the car hobby or the other. In other words, a custom rodder gets to double the fun with one car and give away nothing in the process. Arriving at this happy confluence of styling takes a bit of tightrope walking. It's a high-wire

A little bit hot rod, a little bit custom. Dry lakes–style racing scallops combine with a custom grille bar, tunneled headlights, a shaved bumper, and spinner wheel covers. *Mike Chase*

An early race car–style steering wheel and an aluminum steering-column mount is more typical of a hot rod than a custom, but it works. *Mike Chase*

act, however, that begins with choosing the right car to transform into a custom rod.

Surprisingly, the same car that becomes a classic-era custom is also the perfect starting point for a custom rod project. A 1949 to 1951 Mercury with its top chopped, body dechromed, and fit with a different grille, fender skirts, and side pipes instantly becomes a custom to anyone's definition. With a little rearranging of the parts list and the modifications made, however, that same Mercury—either chopped or with its stock-height roofline unaltered—can

also become a really nice custom rod. The first difference might be the car's stance.

Where a custom is tail-dragging low, a custom rod would be just the opposite. A down-in-back profile is mandatory for a custom, whereas a hot rod is normally set up with its nose lowered just slightly more than its tail. It's an important distinction. This so-called "raked" stance probably got its start during the early days of hot rod racing on California's dry lakes during the 1930s and 1940s. The result was bigger rear tires mounted for higher top

This Cadillac is as classy as a mild custom gets. All the original trim and emblems were left in place.

speeds, and it was also an attempt for a little bit of aerodynamic help. Whatever its origin, the nose-down attitude has been associated with hot rods ever since. A raked car instantly gains an aggressive look. This is something that holds true even when applied to a car that is normally not treated this way, like a 1950 Merc. The next difference would be the absence of the fender skirts and side pipes. Fender skirts don't go with a rake, and hot rods don't mount side pipes, although this is an area open to discussion. Side pipes are also called "lakes pipes," and their original function was a quick and easy way to open up the exhaust system for racing. Over the years they've evolved into more of an adornment, and in many cases, they aren't even connected to the car's exhaust system. A custom rod can still have side pipes, but to be authentic they had better be hooked up and functional. One caveat here might be the length of the pipes. Short side pipes that extend just a little way along the length of the

continued on page 76

A late-model Cadillac's interior has been transplanted, virtually intact, into this early Caddy. The result is eye-catching, and it's also a comfortable ride.

This Sedanette's sloping bodylines and tailfins are classic 1950s. Many customizers choose to leave this look almost stock.

Cool Cruising:

The All-Custom Events of the West Coast Kustoms

There are hot rod, truck, and musclecar events, and then there are events where the emphasis is on one thing only—customs. Not every auto-enthusiast gathering is created equal, and some of them come with side pipes, fender skirts, spotlights, and flame throwers. When that is what you are looking for, a custom-only event is where you need to be.

Custom-car events, usually held over a long weekend at a state or regional park or fairground, are scheduled all over the country and throughout the year. They're great places to see who's doing what, discover new customizing tricks and trends, and get new ideas for customs still under construction. For an idea of just what goes on at one of these candy-colored,

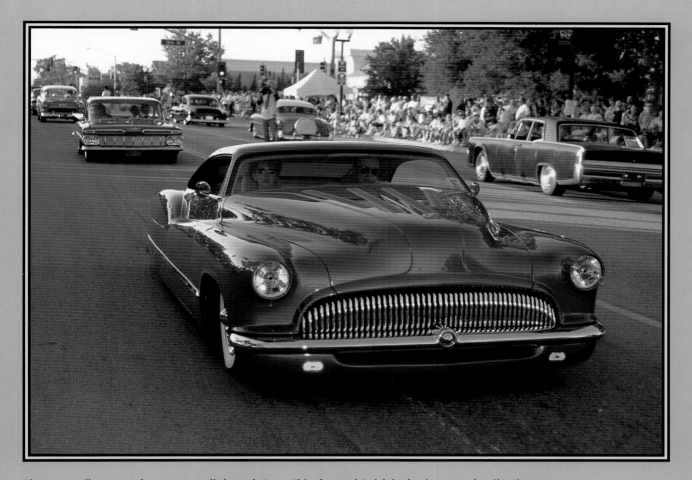

The years roll away as the customs roll through Paso. This chopped Buick is classic-era cool. *Mike Chase*

metalflake happenings, it's useful to focus on just one, and perhaps the most famous and best attended of them all is the West Coast Kustoms' Paso Robles gathering.

Formed in 1982 ". . . for Kustom People . . . By Kustom people," the West Coast Kustoms is a car club that's all about the nifty 1950s, lead sleds, and customs of all styles. The club makes a point of honoring the pioneers of customizing too. As thousands of custom-car fans have found, there's no better reason to

get a custom out of the garage and on the road than to join in on the fun at one of the West Coast Kustoms events. The club hosts four events a year, and the best known is the one held over the Memorial Day weekend in Paso Robles, California.

In the beginning, Paso Robles was strictly a lead-sled deal. Chopped Mercs, bubble skirts, and the words "Daddy-O" painted on the continental kit set the tone. Celebrity guests would be famed customizers

Left: There is nothing like cruising in a panel-painted, 1960s-style T-bird. Paso Robles is a customizer's dream weekend. *Mike Chase*

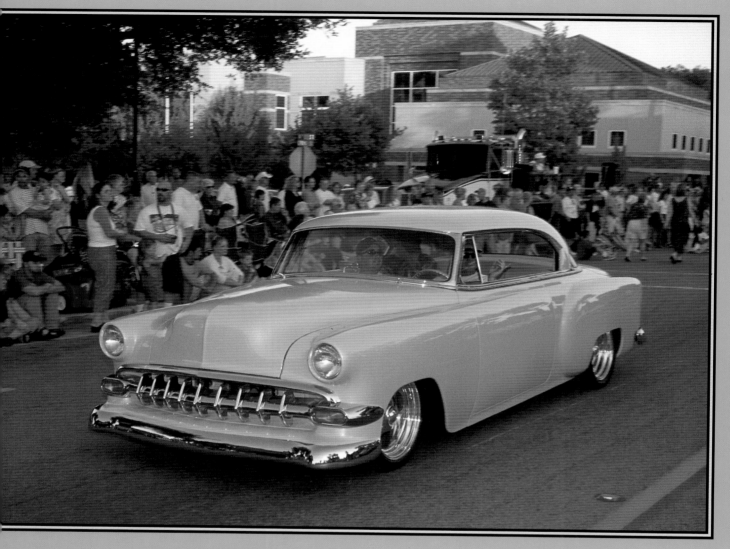

Mild-style custom rods such as this Chevy are cruising standards. This one is as neat as a pin. *Mike Chase*

such as Joe Bailon, Gene Winfield, and Frank DeRosa. For years all this remained a well-kept secret. Now Paso Robles, or, simply, Paso to the in-crowd, is a true festival of customizing.

Cruising Paso Robles, or just walking around taking it all in, is a weekend not soon forgotten. These days the whole town joins in and turns the small coastal community into custom-car heaven. There are organized, full-town cruises, and a show-'n'-shine like none other is set up in the downtown park. There are vendors everywhere selling everything from poodle skirts to hubcaps. There is a lot of great food and live music, and there's even a custom-car fashion show. Paso Robles is a giant car party with a definite emphasis on customs.

The West Coast Kustoms stage an encore over the Labor Day weekend too. More great cruising, show-'n'-shines, vendors, food, and more everything. The club hosts an annual Cruise to the Beach, a custom party with a Beach–Blanket Bingo theme. Every five years the club hosts a Rebel Run to pay tribute to James Dean. It's a cruise that starts from Van Nuys to retrace Dean's fateful final trip.

If all this sounds like fun, that's because it is! A big custom-car event is also a learning experience. It's a classroom that just happens to be as cool as cool gets. Every style of custom is sure to attend, and every custom-car owner there is just waiting to answer questions about how this was done, how that was done, or where that part came from. Just don't forget to bring your Brylcreme!

Wild flames and scallops distinguish this Riviera. It's all part of the Paso Robles scene. *Mike Chase*

The 1949 to 1951 Ford is a custom-rod/mild-custom favorite. Scallops, skirts, and frenched taillights distinguish this one. *Mike Chase*

Continued from page 70
rocker panels might be preferable to full-length pipes, especially full-length side pipes ending with dressy multiple openings capped with cute covers. A custom rod should appear functional, not frilly. To that end, short chrome-plated exhaust cut-out stubs tucked up into the front wheelwells might be an appropriate option. Here are racer-correct pieces that say, "This car is all about go, not show!"

A pair of exhaust cut-outs sneaking out of a custom rod's front wheelwells brings up the next important distinction between a strictly custom car and something else: the choice of the wheels and tires. Full wheel covers and whitewall tires are an integral part of a classic custom's look. Intricate wheel covers like the Oldsmobile Fiesta and Cadillac Sombrero are long-time favorites. Many customs even go

Blending the old and the new. Late model seats, steering column, and steering wheel face a slightly modified, early model dashboard.

so-called "reversed" wheels featuring deep-set rims. Five-spoke mag-style wheels, a traditional wheel-set seen on many hot rods and a direct crossover to a custom rod, are another popular choice. Halibrand wheels are yet another possibility. Getting the picture? The tires mounted up on any of these wheels should and would be hot rod appropriate too. Lately, with the swing to all-things 1950s gaining favor, that could mean wide whitewalls just as easily as it could mean plain black-wall tires. Although the whitewalls would best be used on those chromed wheels or on a set of plain, painted wheels with small center hubcaps. Whitewalls usually don't look their best on five-spoke wheels or mags, but that's not a hard-and-fast rule, either. Remember, there are no rules in customizing!

Now, on top of this basic platform—a nose-down raked stance, a hot rod's wheel-and-tire selection, and an overall no-nonsense appearance—many of the sheet-metal modifications normally applied to a pure custom can be used on a custom rod. This is where the blending of the two styles begins. All of the chrome-trim removal techniques cross right over between both styles, rod and custom, as do things such as hood nosing, decking, and handle shaving. Those are all standard practices in hot-rodding, just as they are in customizing. A custom rod gets to carry this kind

beyond this with aftermarket spinners, flippers, and chrome-plated naked lady sculptures. In place of all this whimsy, the custom rod rolls on a set of traditional hot rod wheels and tires and gives off the air of function over form, although hot rod wheels and tires are by no means formless. They're timeless. Chrome-plated wheels are one example of what might be found on a good custom rod, especially the

Next page: Hood louvers, a "bull nose" hood strip, and polished American five-spoke wheels mark this Chevy as more rod than custom.

of sheet-metal modification even further. It's not uncommon to see custom rods with tunneled headlights; molded and frenched antennas; rounded hood, door, and trunk corners; and complete taillight and taillight-housing replacements. Custom grille work is just as popular on a custom rod as it is on a pure custom, and top-chopping is always allowed. In fact, it's hard to find a hot rod without a chopped top, so there's no reason to exclude that modification here. The main point to keep in mind with any of these sheet-metal modifications is that the end result is meant to look functional and even somewhat aggressive, and not so much streamlined and swoopy as would be the intent with a pure custom.

As already noted, many of the cars open to the custom-rod style are the same cars that also lend themselves to pure customizing. Those 1949 to 1951 Mercs can go either way. The same holds true for same-year Fords and Chevys, indeed for most Fords and Chevys right up to the early 1960s models. If any car can be modified to look a little tough, it's a likely candidate for custom rodding. Conversely, a Lincoln Continental or a later-model Cadillac, Oldsmobile, Pontiac, or Buick could never give up its luxury, big-car style, nor would anyone want it to. Those are the cars best left alone or shifted into a more purely custom realm.

A build plan for a custom rod, aside from the sheet-metal modifications that might be added, to a large part parallels the build process of a typical hot rod. Take, for instance, what might be the case of a typical custom rod, a 1954 Chevy Bel Air hardtop. Beginning at the bottom, the car most likely will have its front and rear suspension completely replaced. A hot rod's Mustang II independent kit is popular for the front, and an aftermarket parallel-leaf rear setup is common. To take the place of the vintage six-cylinder engine, a freshly built and hopped-up 350 small-block V-8, might be

Whether it's a rod or custom, frenched taillights and a shaved trunk lid are appropriate anywhere.

installed. It may even be backed with a four-speed manual transmission. It's all about aggressiveness. The cute, maybe even a little boxy, bodylines will pretty much remain intact and be cleaned up stem to stern to create the perfect blend of rod and custom. The overall effect would be perfect if the car was set low and raked over polished five-spoke wheels, the door and trunk handles shaved, and the hood

bull-nosed and louvered. On the inside, the stock seats might simply be reupholstered in a tight-tuck 1950s or 1960s pattern. It's more hot rod than custom in flavor and flair, but that would be it. Anything more would be unnecessary. Custom rods, the most versatile of all customs, also happen to be among the easiest to craft. It's a win-win situation, and a wonderful way to customize.

Chapter Five

Oakland and Sacramento

Two Top Car Shows in the Custom World

Sacramento is nicknamed "Custom City" because of breathtaking cars like this. Here's an example of customizing to make a car better and not just different. *Mike Chase*

More than 50 years ago, Al and Mary Slonaker hosted a little car show at the Exposition Building in Oakland, California. Today that show is very much alive and known as the Grand National Roadster Show. Along with all the hot rod roadsters and the world-famous 9-foot trophy that is awarded annually to "America's Most Beautiful Roadster," Oakland is also home to some of the best and the finest custom cars in the nation. It's been the same way from the beginning.

The Oakland line runs from Al and Mary Slonaker, who started it all, to Don Tognotti and Show Promotions. It was recently passed on to Dan Cyr Enterprises Inc. The location has switched from that original Exposition Building to the Oakland Coliseum, to San Francisco's Cow Palace, and to San Mateo. The location doesn't matter because the show hasn't changed a bit. It's always been, and probably always will be, "the" place to showcase a custom. Who would have thought that the little car show that began in 1950 would

Setting up for the Big Show. Campaigning a custom on the pro circuit takes real dedication. *Mike Chase*

The main floor at Oakland. For many, displaying their vehicle here is a customizing dream come true. *Mike Chase*

evolve into the world-famous extravaganza it is today?

Typically, an Oakland show will include 500 cars and 100 custom motorcycles. Every one of the vehicles is hand-picked and personally invited. An Oakland quality car is the cream of the crop, and it's an honor to participate, no matter if you win or lose. The six-day show culminates with the traditional Fire Up and Drive Out Night to prove that at Oakland the show cars are "go" cars too.

This is the custom-car show people talk about. It is the oldest, grandest, custom-car show in the country, and every enthusiast should see Oakland at least once. More than that, Oakland is also the show every custom creator dreams of winning. There's no other show that holds out the same amount of status to its winner. From George Barris to Gene Winfield, a list of builders that have been honored at Oakland would read like a who's who in the field. There's even an annual Builder of the Year

The most exotic, hand-formed customs are almost common at Oakland. *Mike Chase*

award, which is a coveted honor to those actually responsible for the construction of the customs on the show floor.

Most of all, Oakland is the custom-car show with history. Fifty-plus years of championship customs under one roof is cause for celebration, and the Grand National Roadster Show is certainly a celebration. It is, and always has been, special.

Significantly, the new custodians of this heritage also produce a number of other custom-car shows, including the Sacramento Autorama. If it's the hot rod roadsters that lead the way at Oakland, customs rule at Sacramento.

From its small-time beginnings in 1950, the Sacramento Autorama has grown to become the Number One custom show in the world, second in overall recognition only to

Did we say the Chrysler Corporation cars offered custom possibilities? The grille and headlight treatment is especially noteworthy here. *Mike Chase*

Oakland. It's been quite a run, and it's far from over!

Sacramento has forged its own identity over the years. Where Oakland is known as the home of the traditional roadster, the Sacramento Autorama has become the premier showcase for customs. With good reason, Sacramento has become the Custom Car Capitol of the World.

The first Autorama was presented by Sacramento's own Harold "Baggy" Bagdasarian. Then-president of the Thunderbolts Car Club, he talked the club into putting on the show. Twenty-two customs were entered and 500 people showed up to see them. Bagdasarian persuaded the guys to try it again, and by the third Autorama, Baggy was on his own and he wasn't looking back.

This is an example of interesting taillight work, and it's typical of what's shown at Oakland. *Mike Chase*

From its headlights to its sculpted side panels and sharply angled tail fins, this is custom metal working at its best. *Mike Chase*

Station wagons are fast gaining favor as customs, and wagons don't come more custom than this Buick. The walled-off display lets show-goers look but not touch. *Mike Chase*

By 1955 the Autorama, now held in the Merchandise Mart Building at the California State Fairgrounds, had grown exponentially, and the 1963 show drew nearly 30,000 spectators. The show moved to an even larger building for 1964, and the number of entries were up to 150. Bagdasarian moved the Autorama once again in 1970, this time to new buildings at the Cal Expo. Entries jumped to 175. Today, the Autorama hosts upwards of 300 cars.

Bagdasarian headed the show all through the 1970s and 1980s, and eventually teamed with another Sacramento businessman, Don Tognotti. In February 1999, Dan Cyr Enterprises

The clever use of paint adds accent to this Cadillac and creates the illusion of added bodylines. *Mike Chase*

A Lincoln Continental is pure custom luxury. Shows like A Lincoln Continental is pure custom luxury. Shows like Sacramento have it all. *Mike Chase*

This is a chopped-top 1957 Chevy Nomad station wagon. Note the careful work around the headlights. *Mike Chase*

Inc. of Portland, Oregon, took over. Cyr, who also produces the Oakland show, has taken the Autorama to new heights.

Over the years, Sacramento has debuted custom classics such as the *Golden Sahara, Golden Sahara II, Platinum LeMans, Kopper Kart, Surf Woody, Mantaray, King T,* and *Green Voodoo.* It has celebrated the work of George and Sam Barris, Joe Bailon, Dick Bertolucci, Boyd Coddington, Sam Foose, Blackie Gejeian, and countless others. The Autorama has established some very special and coveted awards in honor of customizing's pioneers. When Sam Barris passed away in 1967, a

Next page: Here's a real 1960s-style custom grille in a context where it works. *Mike Chase*

This is a 1955 Chevy Nomad wagon. The sloped hood, fenders, and headlights are completely custom. *Mike Chase*

memorial award was begun in his name. It is awarded each year for the best use of metal and paint. Another award was created to honor the Autorama's founder. The Harold Bagdasarian Award for the World's Most Beautiful Custom is presented to a car that features a significant silhouette change, including chopping, channeling, and sectioning. Another premier Sacramento prize is the Joe Bailon Award, for the best use of Candy Apple paint, a Bailon signature. Most recently, the Dick Bertolucci Award for Automotive Excellence was instituted and honors Bertolucci's renowned eye for fit, finish, and detail.

While most spectators have no idea of the amount of work involved in the building of the cars or the preparations required for a show, showing a custom on this level isn't something for the faint of heart. Preparation will involve countless 16-hour days of nonstop work, and it's all for the trophy. There is no question that displaying cars in this fashion is a painstaking labor of love. Elaborate displays are created to show the cars at their best, and some displays end up costing as much as the price of a new car. If it helps in garnering an Oakland or Sacramento win, is it worth it? To a customizer, you bet.

Index

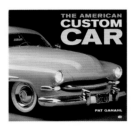

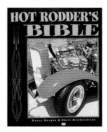
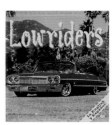